When Life Gets Complicated, Look For
Simple Solutions

When Life Gets Complicated, Look For
Simple Solutions

Dick Sutphen

Other Books By Dick Sutphen

From Simon & Schuster Pocket Books: *You Were Born Again To Be Together, Past Lives/Future Loves, Unseen Influences, Finding Your Answers Within, Earthly Purpose,* and *The Oracle Within.* From Valley of the Sun: *Predestined Love, Past-Life Therapy in Action, Sedona: Psychic Energy Vortexes, Master of Life Manual, Enlightenment Transcripts, Lighting the Light Within, Heart Magic, Reinventing Yourself* and *Radical Spirituality.*

Valley of the Sun Publishing
Box 38, Malibu, California 90265

First Edition July 1996
Library of Congress Card Number: 96-60416
ISBN Number 0-87554-603-X

The concepts in this volume reflect the wisdom of many great teachers. The ideas appear in different forms in Dick Sutphen's seminars and books published by Valley of the Sun and Pocket Books.

If you don't know exactly what you want to happen in a situation, your first priority is to establish clarity of intent, with no indecisiveness whatsoever. This is half the battle.

Forgiveness is often the simplest solution of all (and that includes forgiving yourself).

The simplest solution is often one word: "No."

When your life gets too complicated, give your own interests priority.

Know what you want to accomplish before you start a project.

Don't let what <u>might</u> happen stop you from taking a growth step.

When you make a mistake,
evaluate what needs repairing,
then, start all over again.

If you want something to be different than it is, ask yourself two questions: "If I get what I say I want, what will change?" and "What are the potential undesirable changes?" Any blocks will be found in the answers to the second question.

Never "should" on yourself. Do things because you want to do them, not because you "should."

Break your problem down into pieces, and then work at solving it one piece at a time.

Some tasks don't need to be done. Now or ever. Acknowledge that you don't want to do it, that you're not going to do it. Then the task can no longer drain your energy.

The first step is to decide what you want. The second step will be obvious.

Instead of viewing a problem with another person in terms of conflicting solutions, think of it as conflicting needs. What are your needs? What are the other person's needs? How can you both win?

Good things can have bad outcomes. Bad things can have good outcomes. Rather than jumping to conclusions, wait and see.

When all else fails try being who you really are.

What you leave incomplete
you'll be doomed to repeat.
So, complete your incompletes.

Instead of concentrating on eliminating the stress, concentrate on eliminating what isn't working in your life.

Change has to start intellectually and work it's way down to the emotional level. Next time you are upset, say to yourself, "I'm upset because my expectations are in conflict with what is." This will help diffuse the anger, because you'll have to question your right to have such expectations. At the same time express your angry feelings, clearly, without emotion. In time, with practice, you will begin to allow anger to pass through you without affecting you, because it is the most intelligent choice.

Note: "What is" is an unalterable reality—someone or something you cannot change.

Look at your life and circumstances
from this perspective:
"Does it work for me?" If not,
change is in order.

Don't let your thoughts control your life. If your thoughts disturb you, think about something else. It can be done with conscious effort.

To solve your problem, approach it from a totally different direction.

Sadness is the result of hurt, loss or lack. Beneath the sadness is anger. Explore the anger. Is it justified? If not, give it up. If it is justified, release it by expressing it, before it turns into depression.

One of the
simplest solutions
is to WAKE UP!

Your self-image creates who you are. Change your self-image to change your life. Clue: Self-image results from what you do in life.

When a conflict arises, use your energy to help eliminate the fear. Do not direct your energy against the people or situation—resolve the **fear** and you resolve the conflict.

Growth results from risk, which is a matter of committing to actions you can't control.

To forgive yourself,
you must forgive others.

When you rise above your expectations of others, you negate their ability to upset you.

Blaming and complaining are expressions of self-pity. Accept that you are a co-creator of the undesirable situation, even if you are not consciously aware of your participation.

SIMPLE SOLUTIONS

If you want things to change, you will have to **act!**

You will never attract people more loving than you are. It follows that if you want more love in your life, you have to become more loving.

You only get upset when you don't get what you want. You want others to agree with you, approve of you, or you want to control their actions. To avoid getting upset, accept that other people aren't here on earth to do what you want them to do.

Life gets simple when you want what you get, instead of trying to get what you want.

To release your past you must mourn your loss.

There is never an ideal time, so don't sit around waiting for the perfect conditions. Success comes to those who are bold enough to risk.

The first step to establish a sense of connectedness with someone else is to share who you are.

You create your reality with your beliefs, and it doesn't even matter if your beliefs are true. If you believe something, it becomes true for you. Negative beliefs about self-esteem, body image, career, and romance will become true just as a positive belief will also become true.

To take control of your time you must:
1) Know what to do.
2) Make yourself do it.

We live in an illogical, irrational, unjust world.
That's "what is."
Resisting "what is" won't help.

Accept that there is no way to know the <u>reasons why</u>. In psychological terms, "all symptoms are over determined." In other words, they have more than one cause. Taking this one step further, with any important situation or event, there are multiple causes.

Y ou always have the free will
to choose how to react in
any situation.

Let your words and deeds reflect your real feelings.

Don't spend your time trying to find love. Spend your time trying to remove the barriers you have built against finding love.

You don't have to choose. You can sit back and observe what unfolds. If fear arises, refuse to identify with it. You are not the emotion; you are the observer.

Make immediate sacrifices for long-term satisfaction.

Comparing yourself to others is an inaccurate way of determining value or accomplishment.

Start viewing your problems as decisions that need to be made.

When you've done all you can, continue to be practical, and expect a miracle.

Visualize your future as you would like it to be. You cannot attain what you cannot envision.

No one can change someone else. So, if you are going to allow the other person to remain in your life, you might as well accept them as they are. Your only choices are to fight them being the way they are, or accept them as they are. The outcome will be the same, but acceptance makes life easier.

Your current situation is the manifestation of your beliefs. If you want things to change, you must change your beliefs about who and what you are, and what you need to be happy.

Unhappiness is caused by **self-deception**. How are you hiding from "what is"?

If you're attempting to solve your problem by learning something new, consider unlearning something instead.

SIMPLE SOLUTIONS

There is only a value judgment standing between you and what you desire.

What you call reality is what you've agreed reality to be for you. And you can change it.

You have within you everything you need to be happy in the present. Draw upon your awareness to make the right choices.

You are not your tension or anxiety. These things are just signals that life is not working.

To be happy now, do not compare this moment to any past moments.

Always be assertive, which means to stand up for your human rights. Never be aggressive, which means to violate other people's human rights.

You do not <u>have</u> to react to other people's behavior. Remind yourself of that the next time you're upset.

Ask yourself what is the worst that could happen, and what is the best that can happen?
Be prepared for either outcome.
Then face the situation head on.

What other people say or do, other than physical violence, does not affect you. Only what you think about what they say or do affects you.

Before deciding to do something, ask yourself, "Do I really have the energy for this." If you don't, don't start.

Answers are not difficult when you stop hiding from the questions.

Even when your desires confuse the issue, in your heart you know what to do.

If you seek abundance
you must act as if you
deserve abundance.

Trying to change "what is"
usually doesn't work.
Trying to change how you feel
about "what is" usually does.

The price of being negative to another person is turbulence or disturbance within yourself.

Actions influence attitude.
If your behavior is not serving
you, a change in behavior will lead
to a change in attitude.

A setback is not a defeat.
Try again.

Any problem can be resolved with a change in viewpoint. You can choose the way you view what happens to you.

Relationships based upon need, are based upon how to avoid losing. When you resist loss, you draw it to you.

Your personality is the sum total of all your past programming. It amounts to your traits, viewpoints and habits, and the interaction of these three factors. They are acquired, not inherited. Thus they are alterable.

If you want your life to work you have to set priorities. This begins with the best use of your time, daily planning and long term goals.

If you have nothing to lose,
you can try anything.

Give your all, plus 10 percent.

Fear of expressing your true feelings dissipates your energy. The more you repress, the less energy you'll have to be who you are.

Adaptation is a key to winning.

Before reacting negatively, ask yourself, "Does it really matter or am I just acting out of a need to be right?"

You can only attract what you subconsciously feel worthy of attaining. If you're not getting what you want, it's time to work on your self-esteem.

If you are not as happy and fulfilled as you desire to be, ask yourself, "What at this moment is lacking?"

You always act emotionally. You do what you do because it's what you want to do, and your rationales are nothing but excuses to justify your actions. Make it all right with yourself to act without the internal run-around.

To be in love means, at least occasionally, that you'll experience frustration, anger and emotional pain: When this happens, it is time for you to calmly, honestly and directly communicate your needs.

Never allow another person's words or deeds to influence how you feel about yourself. One has nothing to do with the other.

For life to work you have two basic psychological needs that must be fulfilled. 1) You need at least one person in your life to love and who loves you in return. Without this essential person you will be unable to fulfill your basic needs. 2) You need to feel worthwhile to yourself and others. To maintain high self-esteem, you must maintain a satisfactory standard of behavior and correct yourself when you are wrong. If your behavior is below your standard, and you don't correct it, your life won't work. Now you know what needs to be done.

You often fear what you desire: Friendship, sex, wealth, approval, security. The secret is to be afraid and act anyway.

If you don't have enough time, energy, sex, or success,

STOP WATCHING TV.

If you don't really communicate with your lover,

STOP WATCHING TV.

If your life works,

WATCH A LITTLE TV.

To argue constructively,
agree to avoid these words:

NEVER, ALWAYS, and SHOULD.

You can't be someone you're not. Stop trying.

There are three ways to create change in a human being:

1. Add something: people, things, environment, awareness, responsibility, et cetera.

2. Subtract something: people, things fear, guilt, responsibility, et cetera.

3. Get the person to be who they really are. This is transcendent change.

If you seek success, copy this page and place it on your bathroom mirror, desk, refrigerator, and the dashboard of your car:

"I WILL SPEND EACH MOMENT DOING THE MOST PRODUCTIVE THING I CAN."

When you ask for what you want and the answer is no, LET IT GO!

Don't justify your failures by defending your limitations. Focus upon your possibilities.

You always have a CHOICE as to what you do, who you're with, where you live, and how you spend your time. Sometimes you forget this.

Stop trying to create wrongness in those you're in conflict with.

Take responsibility for your thoughts, words and deeds. It simplifies life.

If your primary goal is peace of mind, decisions become easier.

Mental or physical pain is telling you to do something. Do what needs to be done and the pain will go away.

Your attraction to someone should not be a justification to give them power over you.

When you do something for someone else, it is to fulfill your own needs. Remind yourself of that when seeking appreciation.

You can't become what you resent. If you resent rich people, you'll never be rich. If you resent people who have happy relationships, you'll never have a happy relationship.

You don't have to be in control to survive.

No matter what anyone else says, it's O.K. to: Share your opinions. Ask for what you want. Say no when you want to say no. Say yes when you want to say yes.

If all else fails, quote Jack Kerouac: "I don't know. I don't care. And it doesn't make any difference."

When nothing is really important, people without a life assign importance to unimportant things and make them into a big deal. Even if you don't think you have a life, you don't have to do this.

You have the right to change your mind. What works for you today may not work tomorrow. What you liked last year may not fit with the more aware you of today. Changing your mind is healthy and normal, but other people may resist by challenging your right to do so. They will want explanations and the admission that your first choice was a mistake.
Ignore them.

Everyone; husband, wife, children and friends, think they know how to best spend **your** time.
To attain more freedom, manage your own time.

S elf-discipline is the one factor
common to all self-made
successful people. Self-discipline isn't
about self-denial or self-restrictions.
Self-discipline simply means that you do
what you need to do, and stop doing
what doesn't work.

When you catch yourself thinking negative, say, "positive opportunity." Then replace the negativity with a positive version of the same thought.

When considering an emotional risk, know that it amounts to honestly expressing what you feel.

Ninety percent of success
results from four factors:
ENERGY
ENTHUSIASM
POSITIVE SELF-IMAGE
and DISCIPLINE

Once you know what you want,
you know what to do.

There is always more than one way to get what you want if you'll look beyond the specifics of your desire to the experience the fulfilled desire will create. Then consider all the ways you can manifest the experience.

Stop finding fault and find love.

D o only what you enjoy. DELEGATE to others what you don't want to do. You may have to work a little more at what you enjoy doing to earn the money to pay them. But wouldn't it be worth it?

S eparate your real needs
from your desires.
Then give your real needs priority.

There is no perfect partner waiting in the wings. There is nothing outside of yourself that can fulfill your needs. There is nothing that will last forever. Once you accept these realities you can get on with your life.

Do not let perfectionism block success. If your standards are so high you can't meet them, you'll never accomplish anything.

How someone feels about someone or something is a natural result of their past programming. They feel "right" no matter how illogical it seems to you. The way to win the game is to acknowledge their rightness: "I understand how you feel. I'd like to express how I feel so we can find a way to fulfill both our needs."

If you want to be good at something, you must be willing to spend the time, effort, and sacrifice required to master the ability. Few people are willing to do this. If you are, you're ahead of the game.

You are the only one who can limit your choices in life.

Your resistance to the things you cannot change causes you suffering. If you can't change them, it is truly foolish to resist them. Acceptance sets you free.

(You do realize that you can't change other people don't you?)

It's alright not to be competent
all of the time.

Ask for what you want,
directly and honestly.

Every ending is
also a new beginning.
What potentials does your
new beginning offer?

You do not have to manipulate circumstances. Sit back, relax, and observe what will happen without your interference. If you let events evolve naturally, the outcome may surprise you.

Trying is lying. Just do it.

Continual conflicts destroy a relationship. Occasional conflicts clear the air. Choose your battles carefully.

Change begins with imagination. If you are imagining things other than they are, you have set change into motion. The greater the emotional desire, the sooner the change will take place.

If you're stuck in a game you can't win, maybe it's time to stop playing even if the game isn't over.

No one has the right to expect you to be perfect (not even yourself.) Just do your best.

When your choices are eliminated, your path becomes clear.

Your greatest resource is time.
You either spend it or waste it.
Spending time means using it constructively,
profitably, and ideally in a fulfilling way.
Spending time might be working toward your
success, or a dinner with good friends. Wasted
time would be shared with people you don't
enjoy, or doing busy work without benefit.
We all have the same 1440 minutes a day.
Don't waste yours.

When something isn't right for you,
and you don't act to change it,
you make a choice to accept "what is."

You get eighty percent of your results from twenty percent of your efforts. Simplify, and focus on the twenty percent that's working.

Sometimes the only way to be
responsible to yourself,
is to remove yourself from the
environment you find yourself within.

Where your attention goes, your energy flows. You attract what you concentrate upon. So, concentrate upon positive, loving, successful things.

If you need the approval of others, seek out a successful person you admire.

You are not here on earth
    to fulfill another's expectations.
Sometimes just remembering this
fact helps to put life in perspective.

Aliveness is real enjoyment in doing what you do. It's the joy, stimulation, and pleasure that make life worth living. The best way to generate aliveness is to do what you really want to do.

When you are making choices,
choose what you want most,
not what choice makes the most sense.

You don't have to change anything, and that includes who you are.

ABOUT THE AUTHOR

Dick Sutphen (pronounced Sut-fen) has written several of the all-time best-selling books on metaphysics and reincarnation, including *You Were Born Again To Be Together, Earthly Purpose, Finding Your Answers Within, The Oracle Within,* (Simon & Schuster Pocket Books) *Reinventing Yourself, Radical Spirituality, Predestined Love* and *The Spiritual Path Guidebook* (Valley of the Sun). *Heart Magic* is a collection of Dick's mystical fiction about finding love and answers. Over 100,000 people have attended a Sutphen Seminar. Two hundred Sutphen audio/video tape titles are currently in world-wide release.

The following titles may be purchased at your local New Age store, or you may order them direct from **Valley of the Sun Publishing**. VISA, MasterCard and American Express orders, call toll-free: **1-800-421-6603** or make checks payable to **Valley of the Sun Publishing**. Mail to: Valley of the Sun, Box 38, Malibu CA 90265.